THE MIDDLE AGES

THE
MIDDLE
AGES

Roger Fanning

PENGUIN POETS

PENGUIN BOOKS
Published by the Penguin Group
Penguin Group (USA) Inc., 375 Hudson Street,
New York, New York 10014, U.S.A.
Penguin Group (Canada), 90 Eglinton Avenue East, Suite 700, Toronto, Ontario,
Canada M4P 2Y3 (a division of Pearson Penguin Canada Inc.)
Penguin Books Ltd, 80 Strand, London WC2R ORL, England
Penguin Ireland, 25 St Stephen's Green,
Dublin 2, Ireland (a division of Penguin Books Ltd)
Penguin Group (Australia), 250 Camberwell Road, Camberwell, Victoria 3124,
Australia (a division of Pearson Australia Group Pty Ltd)
Penguin Books India Pvt Ltd, 11 Community Centre, Panchsheel Park,
New Delhi - 110 017, India
Penguin Group (NZ), 67 Apollo Drive, Rosedale, Auckland 0632, New Zealand
(a division of Pearson New Zealand Ltd)
Penguin Books (South Africa) (Pty) Ltd, 24 Sturdee Avenue, Rosebank,
Johannesburg 2196, South Africa

Penguin Books Ltd, Registered Offices:
80 Strand, London WC2R ORL, England

First published in Penguin Books 2012

1 3 5 7 9 10 8 6 4 2

Page 95 constitutes an extension of this copyright page.

LIBRARY OF CONGRESS CATALOGING IN PUBLICATION DATA
Fanning, Roger.
The middle ages / Roger Fanning.
p. cm.
ISBN 978-0-14-312034-6
I. Title.
PS3556.A49M53 2012
811'.54—dc23   2011034502

Printed in the United States of America
Set in Trump Mediaeval LT Std
Designed by Catherine Leonardo

Thank you

Paul Slovak, Jim Backstrom, Heather McHugh,

Brooks Haxton, Kathy Wright, and Henry Fanning

CONTENTS

"When you visualized a man or woman carefully, you could always begin to feel pity—that was a quality God's image carried with it. When you saw the lines at the corners of the eyes, the shape of the mouth, how the hair grew, it was impossible to hate. Hate was just a failure of imagination."

—*Graham Greene*

THE MIDDLE AGES

Fishing for Perch

Fed up with Seattle's coffee jitters, *Star Trek*
fans, and flame tattoos, a semi-Luddite
I tromp my boots on the arboretum boardwalk,

going fishing. I feel better once I'm
squinching a hook through a worm. As for you,
perch, creampuff among convicts, preferring

not to struggle when caught, I'll take solace
from your no más, no más. Meantime, the bobber:
trembles and blips tough to decipher, befuzzed,

like radio signals from Liechtenstein, or moon-bounced
messages on a Ouija board, as waterweeds
go back and forth, back and forth like snoring.

Thus the deadpans of fishermen. Hard to tell
if the two on the bank are friends or not
till one speaks up, and the other laughs so ruefully

I see the chockablock city skyline
as busted teeth, I see the beatitudes'
ruined mouth, as the small fry nibble, undecided.

The Middle Age

Between TV and computer screens
counterfeiting a dragon glow in our mouths agog
and fundamentalists dreaming up real
fire and smoke to transmogrify the U.S.A.,

we may be on our way to something else,
as people in the Middle Ages sensed the decay
of the feudal system. Little orange mushrooms
sprouted from castle mortar and lilies

festered, till BOOM, the Gutenberg Bible
blew the roof off the church. The big party
(individualism) began, and the bare naked
rodeo we now call the Renaissance

gave us—let's face it—the best art ever.
In 1620 F. Bacon posited three
inventions as the high tech hocus-pocus
behind society's sea change: printing, gunpowder,

and the magnet. That's right, the magnet.
Used in compasses, it made heavenly bodies
obsolete, thus exploration of the New
World easy as pie. I mention in passing

Columbus's packs of Mastiffs and Greyhounds
trained on human flesh (brown), but the main
needle that guides my life is the needle
of debt. True North: My Mortgage. I find myself

thinking of Las Vegas, where I might
bathe in lilac neon and wander
palaces, tickled by the bickering
roulette wheels and the final clicks.

And get free drinks. And catch a lion act.
And I would turn my back on all that,
sagely, and walk out in the desert,
letting my crow's feet crinkle ironically.

Out in the desert at sunset
the wind must sequin up a sandgrain
or two, and the prodigal pruneface moon
appear above a dune. Beautiful.

Poignant as hell. And I bet you can hear,
far-off, barking Lotto numbers
the Beast of the Apocalypse. Yes, yes,
a Vegas vacation might be just the thing. Yes,

but I recall my childhood most keenly:
Hansel and Gretel's predicament: luminous
breadcrumbs one by one blinking out, a bird
too dark to be seen.

Possessed of a Red Ryder BB gun, I liked to hunt; that is, I liked to be calmer than usual, watchful in the woods behind our house. We lived near a Navy base, outside which a billboard blared PLEASE PARDON OUR NOISE, IT IS THE SOUND OF FREEDOM. And when the fighter jets of the hellfire decibels did screech overhead, they half-witted the rabbits and birds below. The jets gave you a chance to scuttle within range of any blank-eyed, briefly deaf creature you chose. And in the conspicuous quiet afterward you could aim.

My brain at such times must've resembled one of Uncle Milton's Ant Farms, intricate and busy, only the ants had names like Cruelty and Tenderness and Self-Righteousness—I even thought Cowardice had a part to play—actors in a teeming allegory, let's say. Yes. And how would I now name my actions on a given day, cruel or tender or self-congratulatory? Did I pull the trigger and feel sick at my stomach, or did I not pull the trigger and still feel sick at my stomach?

I refuse to say. I refuse to tell that sort of story. Sometimes the sound of freedom is a loud silence, an angry silence in which the hero sets his stubbled jaw (or his peachfuzz jaw, as the case may be), listening to the hackle-raising roar of untold hormones, my nation's and my own.

Incendiary vs. the CIA's Shoes and "Socks"

(Shoes and "socks:" Is the CIA agent
wearing socks or not? How can one
be ironic about socks? Ask somebody
McHemingway, ask somebody subterfuge.)

Ask the desert dwellers, the most eloquent,
least ironic of people, according to Yeats.
The emptiness of the desert makes
lush their language, an oasis of words.

"Bush the Father and Bush the Son,"
"Bushdog," "Bushpig" the signs in Pakistan
Day-Glo, without irony, bobbing in a mob.
They want George W.'s head on a stick!

But "What is rhetoric but the will trying
to do the work of the imagination?,"
Yeats also says. "Which leads to the work
of the hands," the Book of Job adds.

George W.'s revenge rhetoric begat bravery
and grand debacle. Let's emphasize the bravery.
(And, on an apolitical note, I pray Jesus silence
the voices in my head. They goaded

me to slash a savage confusion of something like
quotation marks into my wrists, apotheosis of irony.)

Fun

Fun to pull the fire alarm.
Fun to have no past or future.
Fun to see a dog with his ears perked up.
Fun to PITY THE BATHTUB.
Fun to discover the coelacanth.
Fun to say "bullet shit."
Fun to thunder, fun to lightning.
Fun to fork, fun to spoon.
Fun to garbanzo bean.
Fun to taste the bluewhite breastmilk.
Fun: fellatio!
Fun: cunnilingus (a little less fun).
Fun to hear sounds the deaf make during sex.
Fun to pop a bottle of bubbly.
Fun to refute Satan's sibilance.
Fun to phone.
Fun to e-mail (a little more fun).
Fun to see the Trailblazers without headbands
(I know headbands mean something bad).
Fun to thumbsdown, fun to boo.
Fun to watch Godzilla wade, dripping water.
Fun to hallucinate: a Tengu swooping out of the trees.
Fun to see Jesus on the undersides of my eyelids
(Jesus always tells you the truth).
Fun to bamboozle.
Fun to fondle the voodoo doll in the likeness of mom.
Fun to find with a flashlight the treed raccoon.

Caul Me Ishmael

It was a motion always in my mind,
sex, the summer I was going insane.

Pornography is a hot dog eating contest in Pompeii.

Catcalls for the first black champ.

I remember Eddie Vedder saying on the radio "it tasted like a
popsicle that had been up somebody's ass."

Hesitant, homoerotic poems about horses and the ocean
and that sort of thing I cannot write.
I have to hetero and be bold.

Language remembers. People forget.

I like looking at clouds in a blue sky,
the white puffy kind.
Clouds make me feel like I'm already dead.

Godlets swimming on a microscope slide.

I always wish to be precise as, inside
a glass ball that magnifies it,
a hair from the beard of Mohammed.

Mr. Fix-It must one day face the Sphinx.

Inside every walnut a gargoyle waits.

Pontius Pilate fish did not fear God the shark.

Faith and begorrah, a plague of frogs
on all the Steadfast Edsels of the City.

God Trumps Beelzebub (Among the Other Bad Angels) Who Drove Me to Suicide in 2004

Chances I took with my life
when I was young: playing
in a gravel pit, driving drunk,
not using a condom. I also
drank water out of a mountain stream
once. . . .

Many years went by
prudently.

Then what?

One summer night I saw a gargoyle
numinous on the peak of our roof. He turned and stared
malevolently over his shoulder at me, a premonition of
the evil tongues, the destruction to come
(also, I could smell cowshit, though I live in a city).
Devil Ibex Horns, Batwings, the Whole Bit:
the Evil One at his Most Dramatic.
I lay very still in my bed.
I was not unimpressed.

(And now a lyrical essay about trying
to be a better person:
I used to worry about the Orangutangs in Borneo.
I used to worry about the future of the rain
forest because of big bad McDonald's.
I used to listen to Murmur over and over.
I still love the warm voice, I still love
the kudzu-crazy vacant lot, I still love the way
the album's best phrase acknowledges a passion
the opposite of most pop songs': "Get away from me.")

2004, the Fall following the Gargoyle Summer,
a coyote-craven frenemy of mine
(who, unbeknownst to me, wanted
to steal my wife) gave me a dose of LSD
on a piece of dark chocolate. Just like
that a crack spread across the van's windshield
but I enjoyed intensely the vivid orange October
foliage, the cold air, the quiet save for our
crunchy bootsteps, that hike in the mountains.
At the end of the trail the Coyote
Trickster wheeled viciously, snarling at me:
"Women cheat, she's gonna be gone."

He had already dropped by the house a couple DVDs:
Pray for Death and *Faces of Death*.

And yet more hatred was to come my way.

Two days after the hike the Peanuts character Linus
from the band Mountain Con got belligerent
in class, castigating me for being
a soft-spoken teacher.
He kept barking the word
"ambiguity." He would not shut up.
When he returned to his seat, he
sat there glaring at me, his chest heaving.
By that time I was insane;
nonetheless class continued.
Eventually a lumpy young woman in a trenchcoat,
Cat, made a cryptic remark
about another teacher's stuttering, or my son's
autism, or Russell Edson's essay on silence,
or all of the above:
"the handicap of language." Like I said
I had gone insane.

Perhaps Linus had lost his mind
too. Cat seemed deliberately acidic.

Three days after the hike
my life became a shrieking visual confusion
synesthesia off and on
(my brain a pet store full of electric green
parakeets panicked by a thunderstorm).

Three nights I had lain awake holding a knife.
Once I saw a sultriness: my wife crouching like a lioness
beautiful but threatening beside me in bed.

Suddenly the urge to light three candles in the bathroom.
Donald Trump, he with the redblond rat's nest on his head,
pooched his mouth out on TV, as if pondering
the Sorcerer's Apprentice. I was frantic to get in the tub.
I was terrified two G-men in an Oldsmobile
would frogmarch me outside and put me in the trunk
and elsewhere torture secrets out of me.
They would sport blond crewcuts
and wear latex gloves and be subtle
when it suited them, then brutal.
Goodbye, goodbye to aluminum siding.
Goodbye, son. Hello, dead parents.
I washed down all the pills I could find
and I cut both my wrists with my dead
father's trusty short sharp fishing knife
(still keen for cutting heads off trout).
Blood left me, bathwater my shadowself.
Pure opera, pure bullfight.
Thrown red roses. Bravo,
bravo middlebrows.

Then two weeks at Harborview with its intermittent
terrors and its glittery astringent smell. At night medication
made my lips so dry they flaked like fishfood, as if
I were a timelapse human sacrifice. Every morning I recalled

a grad student who had written a poem about my son
flapping his hands in the back yard.
How did that student know about my secret pain? Why
such cruelty in the duchy of dactylic
stabitty stab stab? The less

said about it to the hospital staff
the better. I stonewalled them as best
I could, as if I were a zombie POW
in a neverending horrorshow where the walls
each night get carpeted with brindle fur
and the grounds put on a pelt of diamonds. . . .

At last the powers-that-be let me go home
to my wife Kathy (affectionate, she of
the grilled cheese sandwiches and soup and sex)
and then our son Henry home from school
(a little skittish of my scars, underfed,
fat-lipped), and my life too sweet,
at least that day, to be
bedeviled or believed.

Noir Fog Outside the Fright Wig of the Bright Franchise

A beach town in the offseason where fog
allthumbs everything ashore
and radio stations fade to sand:
that's the destination I had in mind.

In my rented Pontiac Grand Prix (black),
I motored dreamily to town for a burger
and fries, my face faintly green, a tad
malevolent from the dashlight.

I had scribbled all day, spoken to no one.
A writer-in-residence type deal.
My treatise on loneliness will begin
with a riddle: hagridden/raghidden,

get it? The answer's what they used to call "self-abuse."
I sat in the parking lot gobbling my food.
In the Playplace a magenta slidetube mimicked
the birth canal, from which children shot out.

A bespectacled chunky cheerleader
in a blue and white uniform laughed
her head back, braces glinting,
because the Willapa Bay Wolves had won

the big game! It was crowded in there,
the rest of town dead. Center stage
a man who looked like me sat
with his family (wife, two boys),

and the youngest one, the tenderest face kept looking straight up,
as though his birthday balloon had escaped. I understand,
I understand that such bright franchises are what pass
for magic in out-of-the-way places everywhere,

and sometimes I think America is just this wreckage
I saw rumbling along in an electric wheelchair once,
a pasty guy wearing a black leather jacket
the hottest day of the year, sweating hard.

The sign on the back of his chair said BEYOND REPAIR.
And once I saw dead, dried-up, wings-askew
birds suspended in jars of clear red gelatin—
detritus handled gently—and lit from behind,

throwing Gothic shadows. It looked like they were soaring.
Put it another way, Ronald McDonald
makes a spooky mascot, but those french fries
do taste good, especially good

in a beach town in the offseason
where fog allthumbs everything ashore
and radio stations fade to sand, to surf,
to the white noise of a wheelchair's motor,
and birds fly south with their bones sticking out.

I.

The Oglala aquifer's dwindling to one
damp white salamander underground,
born without eyes, North and South Dakotas'
townships doomed, the cuckoo clock

about to cuckoo. No aquifer, no people.
But the buffalo can lap from puddles
and lakes, so there's the quixotic notion
of a Buffalo Commons: post office towns,

family farms abandoned, the buffalo
shambling their shaggy tons of shoulders
wherever they pleased, scratching their rumps
real slow against fenceposts, rust-ravaged

Cadillac fins, munching rain-warped porno mags,
yawning hugely. "The 150-year settlement
of the Great Plains is an experiment
that is drawing to a close," the op-ed page

crows. "It is time to be bold." "Again," it neglects
to say. Let another bold experiment begin,
though it's not clear where we'll herd the Indians
this time, reservations being states of mind

as well as places. Besides, I know what it feels like
to wander off the map of America, to let
my country forget me as I return the favor.
Forgive me, I feel rich in nowhere places

when I come across Old Nobody's domiciles,
entranced. I worked as a gofer in the galled employ
of a handyman named Ed, both of us behested
by Century 21 agents in those mustard coats.

Ed and I readied ramshackle houses for rent
or sale, working fast, slapping up paint, an antic
yet morose guerilla warfare against decay,
lassitude setting in. Coffee. Doughnuts. Low pay.

The real estate agents chewed spearmint gum
and used too much cologne, and I shrank under
the fluorescent lights, the whole hale-fellow-well-met
ambiance of the office, but I felt giant,

strong in empty barns. And once an empty house—
we'd been sent there to replace a frozen pipe—
lo and behold, a house with a goat
parading around inside. A real goat. I saw

the beast pass from room to room, clippetyclop,
serene of his domain as the Devil himself.
Stubs of horns and pupils rectangular I beheld.
Spooky. Alien. Italics not mine. The sound

of a goat stutterstepping up a flight of bare wood
stairs is not something you forget, nor the sound of said
goat mincing like a dominatrix above your head,
funny and freaky and foreboding all at once.

(Plus, I had just seen *The Exorcist*.
That may have been a factor. Laughter
from the audience, when things first started
getting hinky, then no laughter.) I found pristine

Twinkies, still in their wrappers, in a kitchen drawer. It's
nasty magic some people leave behind, hoodoos
mute like doll eyes, mirror shards. . . . Goats and Twinkies and
out in the barn a bunch of frozen chickens. . . .

So I'm all for a Buffalo Commons,
or mostly for. It will be the Mystery,
many times over, of the Devil Goat House,
an enigma twittered by a Twinkie wrapper,

a new world seen through a veil
of cellophane, altered, enlivened,
and inside a dead traffic light,
bobbing slightly, three bird nests. . . .

It will be storybook, in the manner
of the Brothers Grimm: both just (to the buffalo
dusty on the comeback trail) and brutal
(to the Indians and the farmers come a cropper

at last). As for the drab specifics
of the chickens left to freeze in the barn,
russet-feathered, unpicturesque, they're
the opposite of a bold experiment,

the opposite of slaughter. They died by degrees,
clunking to the floor like upholstered stones,
their owners chugging away in a station wagon
burning oil, kids in the back. Nighttime. Nothing said.

    II.

In the idiom of Ed such behavior's
known as "chickenshit:" cowardly, inexcusable.

And Ed the Vietnam vet was chickenshit too.

He used to sniffle telling me about his wife
in her wheelchair, but more often he walrus-wheezed

regaling me with tales of infidelities
overseas, Filipino prostitutes, thatch huts,

jungle. "Roger, do you know what a 'foamy' is?
Two naked women covered with soapsuds. . . ."

Untold stories of ruin there, like celluloid scorching through
on a projector bulb then flailing, but here is what

I know: Ed would sum up the best and the worst
of his existence, the true love with a legstump

and the softsoaped women, the flushest paydays
and the near-electrocutions, the same way: "Well, fuck me

to tears" (which I far prefer to the more common
expression "fuck you"). I pledge allegiance to

the best and the worst of us, words and deeds.
That's my credo crumb. Every day the sun rises red,

bloodshot as a drunkard's eye, but it's then that roosters
make a ruckus of the world. They raise, they rose

the rooftops. They do not mutter, fading
inwards. Better to squawk like the stupid, proud

bird you are. Better, all in all, to brag about getting
a foamy, to dye your hair red (as Ed's wife did

to whet the eye), to wear a bright coat
and loud cologne, to raw your throat

with a rube's opinions, a confidence man's
op-ed rhetoric. Better to pretend

you are brave. But then
go home to a riddled house, which is

yourself, who is often estranged
and quiet and gray.

Beowoulfian Bathos of Halvor and the Trolls

General fucked-uppedness of family life,
General vacuity of advertising,
General woundedness. . . .

Great joy in exorbitant stories
because the suggestments of language, shady,
glare into commands.

Oh, those owlish fellows of All Souls College
with their index cards, descendants of
the absentminded moustachioed Manbeast in the Mead Hall
who looks like me, beery, boondoggled. . . .

Best of all stories:
A beautiful woman, who looks like no one else.
White skin, black hair, red lips:
Black crow, red blood, white snow.

Christmas Eve. A man is taking a white bear on a leash to the
King of Finnmark as a gift, through a forest of black sticks. The
man comes to Halvor's cabin, beside which Halvor is chopping
wood.

"Can I spend the night in the cabin?"
"No, the Trolls are coming."

Nonetheless, the man sleeps standing up in a closet. The white
bear sleeps under the table. Party in full swing, party of long-
nosed trolls, long-tailed trolls, trolls all sizes, the white bear
smells sausages cooking and stirs in his sleep. White fur, a move-
ment. Hmmm. . . . A little long-nosed troll with a sausage on a
big two-pronged fork, friendly, approaches the sleeper. "Here,
puss puss." The white bear roars out, scattering the Trolls.

A year goes by.
Halvor is chopping wood in the side yard.
A voice from the woods calls out.
"Hey, Halvor, do you still have that big cat of yours?"
"Yes, and she has seven kittens that are all much larger and more ferocious than she is."
A pregnant silence. The Trolls never take over Halvor's house again.

How did the visits begin? I imagine
the Trolls threatened, merely by
their presence, to hurt Halvor.
What if there is one Heaven and the Trolls are there?
Imagine that: a Heaven that cannot be endured.

There's a house.
There's a wood.

Black Sticks, White Snow, No Blood.
The story would be more beautiful if there were blood.
Halvor should spill the Trolls' blood,
I would.

Photo of Elvis, Salamander Phase, 28 July 1954

All salamanderish and moist is Memphis in July and August, and Elvis himself looks a little moist in this photo. Everything about him's odd, from his crewcut to the piping on his cowboy suit. He's got acne too. He's in-between, amphibious: not quite the poor kid from Tupelo—he's taken to wearing eye shadow, for one thing—but not a star yet either. He's already recorded his vibrato version of "Blue Moon;" he's yipped at the end of "Mystery Train." In other words he's still doing his best stuff. He listens to Dewey Phillips on WHBQ late at night. Surely, when this photo was taken, the night must've smelled of the Mississippi. Was there a dead catfish the size of a Cadillac upriver? The smell must have been heavy, humidity-borne, of diesel-tainted algae blooms, of the aforementioned dead catfish, of wet coffee grounds/newspapers/peanut shells, of sewage, of tropical fruit. Poor fucked-up Elvis, doomed to overflow his sequined jumpsuits, to wreak havoc on his health, to break a woman's ankle while demonstrating his karate skills. After considering the facts of his life, I'm left with the Big Muddy. Such fecundity. Such a mess.

Walpurgisnacht Hospital as Punishment for (Among Other Things) My Racism, Sexism, and Homophobia

Porno scenarios presented themselves
then nothing happened. From the hall
I saw a young black man stripping
out of his pajama top and I thought
he was pretty. I thought "Hey, maybe
I'm gay or (as the ads say) 'bi-curious.'"
A nurse gave me a rather tender
neurological exam, and when my penis stirred
in the thin pajamas, she left abruptly.
A woman who seemed to be a dumbed-down,
less attractive version of my wife murmured
"Do me" in passing. I paced the halls.
Faces unfroze when I glanced at them,
conversations began as I walked by.
I thought I was being punished
for staring at asses, strangely
enough, so I kept my eyes up. Also strange:
I envied the neckhair of one male nurse
who walked ahead of me. It was plush
as sheepswool, unlike mine, which scraggles.
Anti-psychotics made the hospital "The Wizard of Oz:"
Everyone reminded me of someone
else, or an aspect of myself, or
a reproach from a higher being.
I watched a basketball game with
a black man about my height. One
morning a nurse drew some blood
and I made a joke. She said
"That's a good one" and smiled.
Her face seemed to be a vision
of what's best in the world, simple
as the full moon. And I dimly remembered

a face from my diaper days: Ida,
the woman who took care of me
one day a week. Secondhand
I got a story from my mother: the KKK
chained Ida's neighbor to the bumper
of a car and dragged him screaming
up and down the road, more or less skinning him
alive. People sat in their houses,
listening to the screams, terrified.
Then it was quiet. On a walk outside
I saw a seagull land by a red light
glowing on the hospital, I thought it was Satan
showing me his wingspan.

Evil Fairy, Confident Guy

In the hospital I stared at the scars
on my wrists, as though I might levitate. . . .
The blood had flowed freely from my left
wrist, snaking around my arm, then
slowed to a drip. Stopped. (Thanks, God.)

I saw drops of blood on the bathroom floor,
the dog licking them up. Eventually I heard
voices in my head (all negroid at first,
soothing and seemingly truthful as the blues
by Son House, encouraging me
to have sex with my wife—as if

they wanted to watch—then a mix of
humorous voices, some homos, some women,
increasingly scary, mocking the world, my
stream-of-consciousness with sewage).

Punchline to a joke from childhood:
"It was sewerside."

The two most distinctive voices I
nicknamed: Evil Fairy, Confident Guy. "For I am
talking to Roger Fanning." Confident Guy
always starts with "for," Charlton Hestonesque.
Evil Fairy laughs, slapping her forehead in astonishment.

Then came the voices I was afraid
to name: voice of God, voice of the Devil
telling me I was in Hell. Eating sounds.
"You might as well pray to Batman,"
one voice said. Then came the images:

a man and a woman doing it doggy
style, Jesus sticking out his tongue
at me, a guy kicking his heel up
to mime the medicine "kicking in." It

happens when I'm lucky: a dreamless
delicious Lithium sleep comes over
me. Or God intervenes. Or (excuse
the cliché, I'm sick) the big cat
Nick gets tired of teasing
a mouse (me).

My Madness: Sick Minutiae, Ecstasy

Madness: a realm of microflora,
microfauna faunistically speaking
to me, creating in me
hard-to-describe feeling states,
loathing, queasiness. . . .

sex slave cabins wherein
the couches grow monstropoulos arms
(gracias, Zora Neale Hurston)
and hold you down
and the lights go out. . . .

Meanwhile, on occasion I
experience
the Aurora Borealis as music, an
inhuman ecstasy rushing over me.

That is Heaven: tears
rolling into my ears.

This is Hell:
its little animals, its little words
scrawling all over
my unhoused psyche.

Smooth Face

After the calm of her prayer (silent)
came the real raw: she looked up at me
all Bedlam-eyed, abruptly,
my mother. . . . Snowfall rushing

a vast and audible
sibilance around the hospital. . . .
Streetlamps, funnels of light
furiously in reverse: vortices

vetoed by the picayune
squeak of nurses' shoes,
cardio-beeps. . . . My mother
looked up at me

wildly when I walked in,
snow on my coat, because
the past and the future skein
their faceted, nipped-at uniques

hissing like a pit of snakes, as if
to whip an old woman's face.
She knew something, her skin was so smooth.
That's when she looked up, afraid of me.

Bamboo Shadows

(A Godforsaken, ghosty place
where bamboo clatters. . . .
A courtyard in Japan
where I've never been. . . .
Lafcadio Hearn, I find your simple ghost
stories—after your turgid journalism
about murders and suicides—
good.) I'm home. I see
bamboo shadows shifting on a real
wall: baby faces mostly, balloon-like,
not beautiful, a funny view of the foot
of a bed, the feet of two people
having sex gently, in a swimmy way. . . .
All's awkward, off-kilter. . . .
It's not all bad, hallucinating,
not this summer evening the second
year of my years of sickness.
I sit alone in the living
room, in awe of what my mind
and the world—with God
in the mix—have to give.
I had a friend who had about ten
pounds of long black hair, and her long black hair
got hot in the back yard sun.
She taught me how to make a boat
out of a bamboo leaf,
folding it just so (I forget how).
Once I saw a spot of blood on a bamboo leaf.
Once my friend made me cupcakes.
Once she sneezed like a cat.

"Naked into the Next World"

The title refers to a plucked chicken.
The poet's notion of the afterlife
allowed for chickens. His name: Koon Woon.
Hometown: Aberdeen, same as the famous rock star.

(Thick glasses, graying hair) Koon Woon read his well-made
poems to a workshop gaggle of undergrads
(smell of chalk, one dead earwig on the windowsill)
many, many years ago. He wrote THE TRUTH

IN RENTED ROOMS. Friend, unlucky like you,
I prefer to make do
with what I remember: fragments, shards. . . .
They indicate a vase perfectly intact

elsewhere. Maybe you've seen a vase with crazelines,
shakily repaired, dusty on a thrift store shelf?
Glorious its chthonic birth. And if I sound
rattle-brained, it's because I'm older now.

I'm not sure about the next world, I've been
busted to pieces by betrayals/deaths.
I need unguents for an endless gluejob, I crave
to record a few important lines.

You lived alone, and wrote fondly
of the goldfish you'd bought at Woolworths': "It pleases me
with a trail of bubbles." You told yourself:
"There was no conspiracy against a poor man."

"And if I am strong, it is because
my grandmother drew a circle on my back."

(Adhesive is how it begins. Things I hear
and things I see stick in my mind
like Post-its from another world.

I'm subject to fugue states:
a lost feeling, no past or future, when
and where everything refers to me.) One

day I may wake up in a hammock
in Tahiti, with the ghost of Marlon Brando
(no sex). He'll instruct me in the ways of

heartbreak and humiliation:
he became obese (like me) eating peanut butter,
he wore an apron and a dress in one movie,
his son Christian (heavy irony) killed

someone. Great thing Marlon did,
buried in a bad movie, is play
the piano fortissimo (not ridiculous).

He's wearing an umbrella on his head,
zinc oxide on his nose (ridiculous).
Then the camera widens out. There's a 3-foot man

atop the grand piano, sitting at a little
piano, matching the mad scientist
note for note, playing his heart out.

Then it stops. A look of great tenderness
(smiling, about to cry) comes over
Marlon's face. He embraces

the twisted little version of himself
proudly, lovingly. I play it over and over.
I'm all alone, it's late at night: that's about

as hard as I laugh in my whole life.

(Next morning I play it for my wife
and it's not as humorous as I remember,
but she smiles indulgently for her lonely husband.

And now we have a son.)

Canis Major's Countless Morphs of Snout and Mood

I.

Q. "What's the difference between having a Chihuahua and a pit
   bull on your leg?"
A. "You let the pit bull finish."

And so, like a Victorian author
with a waxed moustache, mindful
of the lapdog's burden, I consider
ending this simply THE END

but I opt for the even more
cornball THE END (question mark),
a la a horror movie in which
the serene-at-last dead werewolf's face

and hands unhirsute to human, pale
hairless skin, a mainstream hymn
to vulnerability, and who's the real victim here
anyway? That's just the kind of guy I am.

"Can't we all just get along?"
I wish the post-beating Rodney King
had pled instead "Can't we all
just get alone?"

II.

I remember a weiner dog
with a German Shepherd's big head, chimera of
the neighborhood. Well, my parents were an odd
pair too. Look how my brothers and I turned out.

III.

Timberwolves over time
whelp Chihuahuas, it's true.
We like the cutes.
We give them food.

Dogs, all breeds, follow us.
Dungeaters, thus trainable.

But a cat is a cat is a cat.
No pack, no Pax Romana. Every cat body
compact, cat-like.

"A cat may look at a king,"
Rudyard Kipling wrote. Apt quotes
are bon bons I scarf, always
with a sense of the pack, its
hierarchy, wanting to improve myself,
to move up, woof woof. (Better phrases
than "barbaric yawp?" Naw.) But enough unleashings
and beggings and bared fangs.

Enough ugly dogs in the wake of their masters.
More cats.

Caravaggio's *Sleeping Cupid*, the Wing That Alters Everything

Gut like a beerguzzler's,
gap between his front teeth
(yellow), his skin also yellow. . . .

Full-lipped Caravaggio, you shockmeister,
there are three distinct stages
to my perception of your painting:

the Hallowe'en Stage, in which
I notice the dramatic yellow and black;
the Queasy Stage, in which

I notice the grotesque manchild's
uneasiness in sleep, and suffer
indigestion with him; and the Illumination

Stage, last of all, in which I notice
the lit curve of the wing
that alters everything. . . .

That wing is why so many otherwise gentle people
like to get smacked on the ass
sometimes, after they get bored with tendernesses.

The lit wing that alters everything is why Shakespeare
stuck the last two lines on all those admirable sonnets of his.
Honestly, Mr. Homoerotic,

we all are gluttons,
sensation hogs, angels,
ironical as Shakespeare

(yes, he existed) and his
understudy Rod Serling,
who stood 5' 4".

Caravaggio, synonymous with dissipation, you
should know I love your painting about love
because I am so sick myself.

Most Instructive Scene in *Midnight Cowboy* and a Few Questions for a Man with an Unexplained Black Eye

Midnight Cowboy: A movie about friendship
and domesticity, a sense of normalcy
amid degrading circumstances. . . . Remember
the scene where a woman runs a rubber
rat over her son's face? Remember the scene
where the hustler Joe Buck slams
a phone receiver into a gay priest's face
repeatedly? The priest is on his knees. Bloody,
he pleads, "Thank you, Joe. Thank you
for helping me be good."

I have two questions
for an acquaintance,
he of the absinthish
1890s style dissipation:

Is that a mouse—a purple
half-moon—under your left eye,
seedy 33 year-old former
lead singer for Truth Decay, graduate
of the London School of
Economics, sans health insurance?
Did the waterstained Beardsley wallpaper
peel like Scripture shredding?

Not much sense in letting people
hurt you—I don't anymore—
I keep making jokes
that only I get
and hurt no one:

Go rouge your Punchinello.
Go pee in a shoe.

Swandive

The Minotaur (whisper whisper) has a drinking problem.
But Listerine-scented throaty invocations (his mother's

wheedling, wooing) have keelhauled him clear of
the Labyrinth. Think of all the green bottles there

still glinting like the jaws of mantises, machine-tooled,
precise. Look up the etymology of "cryptic"

if you like. The bottle used to watch out
for you. And here's the changing of the guard:

"Zeus, grant me the courage to swank myself
in swanliness, white feathers, webfeet,

the works; the wisdom not to ask permission
ever, no matter what I need to do;

and the serenity to hide,
undiscoverable, in the sky."

Road Trip

"There isn't a straight line in the world," Heather McHugh
once said. And Paul Klee rightly claimed

that "Drawing and writing are fundamentally
identical." And Kathy Wright cherishes

her mole. Her mother pressured her
to have it removed, but Kathy

drew the line, figuratively speaking (literally,
she ended with a dot), whereas a cartographer

traffics in actual lines (dots too), omitting maybe
a cul-de-sac, maybe a toxic creek. He makes

a mistake to wink at the way things really are, so
his work can then be copyrighted—sold—

because cartography, like Kathy Wright
sanctifying her mole, is ultimately a practical art.

Was Zeno being practical when he supposed
a line is made up of an infinite number of points?

No, but Roethke was: "Lust fatigues the soul."
Also Mishima: "Lust inevitably

attaches itself to fragments." So if
you've driven all day, pondering trade-

and beauty marks and map minutiae
and Andy Warhol's soup cans and the endless

implications of mass production, it's then
that the blue blue information signs

positively sing of GAS FOOD LODGING
and you feel invisible, enchanted, lost:

flawless, if you know what I mean.

Prague

There's a spic-and-span café/venue
of stainless steel and polymers
where homesick Americans can go,
watch a little MTV, hear a Coke fizz:

an antiseptic respite from history
in the hard orange chairs
George Jetson favored.
The crooked sidestreets of the Jewish

ghetto put me in mind of doctor
and nurse appurtenances, deathbeds, Kafka
skeletal, coughing. A man wakes up
as a bug, worried about being late

for work. Kafka thought such stuff
was funny; today most people
don't. I'm in the minority.
I'm with Kafka, but it is horrible to hear

the small fry burrow, undermining your
home; to build the Great Wall generation
after generation; to assemble toggle switches
for Honeywell (something to do with rock-boring

bombs for Afghanistan, maybe, this piecework
farmed out by the military-industrial complex).
Simple: lots of dog doodles on the sidewalks
(no scoop laws in Prague), and the whipped lard

confections the bakeries offer look much
the same. People eat them anyway.
Hardcranny Castle: a statue in dramatic
silhouette, a giant about to bring the cudgel down,

braining an innocent. Cruel? No. It's sweet,
it's Keatsian when history stops forever.

Shine and Sheen

Large-eyed as an embryo, hard-boiled (sort of),
Raymond Chandler's haiku-prone second cousin

twice removed, I don't mind the rain. The rain
sounds like a bony old uncle blown in from Borneo

to do a softshoe on the roof, wanting
a cup of tea, a story. And the black ink voice

in the book I'm reading seems the voice of my
most ungenerous self, industrious but pipsqueak. It

almost dissuades me from the rain, the shoes
shined as for a funeral; I mean the sheen of art

life everywhere, furtively, begets (that is, fashions,
trends, jadedness), also the green-begetting

wet helterskeltering in rivulets, in
fan-shaped rills, in hands. Sheen

shore mezmers me. Lulls like these, the black ink voice
blurs to black ants, rank and file in disarray, haywire,

devoid of crumbs to Hercules up, of hidey
holes, of meanings. Their kind, my love, cannot get in.

Brusheaters

Scotch Highland cattle, imports, now banned
because of Mad Cow Disease, but in my youth
precursors to llamas and emus and other warm-
blooded whatnots bought as emblems

of cool—like potbellied pigs later on,
nevermind Michael Jackson and his Neverland
Ranch, the chimpanzee and the bones
of the Elephant Man—these cows, low-key

novelties within the means of any Navy man,
tattooed and retired, whose spread included
a patch of woods (through which
no path). Useful:

Brusheaters. They foraged in the understory.
Shaggy redbrown beasts with wide curvy horns,
they suggested shrunk-down Woolly Mammoths.
Ominous, but with a hint of affability around

their almost-hidden sheepdog eyes (eyes
outlined like Cleopatra's, except in pink).
Often they blinked as if perplexed. I learned
much from them. Their nettle-stung
mouths they must've numbed in galvanized troughs

(not a speck of rust on them, no
toadspawn in) and pools in the woods
no one bothered to name.

Am Among the Ankle-Bending Beach Stones

Among the ankle-bending beach stones
and sun-bleached beer and soda cans,
it startled me (like parting weeds
to find two leprechauns fucking
on a pile of gold doubloons) to flip

a starfish and see its mouth wibble-
wobbling a mussel shell, mushing
the shard to bluegray goop. *Fuh, shi*:
I made a sound that was half a curse,
my hand jerked back, a buoy clonged.

(Remember the story of the Sleeping Beauty?
The starfish maw smooched me awake, just so.
And by telling the ugsome tale to my wife
later on, I could be the prince who fought
the hedge of thorns, and startle her awake.

But I may have more in common with old
wart-on-her-nose, the thwarted one, who counts
her hours as dead flies upon a windowsill,
who prizes stillness and study most of all.
I yawned as if to swallow a pumpkin.)

A gray man upon a gray beach, once he savors
a starfish funny as appendicitis, gently
sets it right, and trudges on: fussbudget,
footsore, and fleetingly extinguished of
his shine of face, his share of the treasure.

No self-serve pumps in Oregon. State lawmakers understand the importance of an oily rag (salmon-colored, more often than not) hanging from an attendant's back pocket, and the importance of a tire pressure gauge, with its reassuringly tiny increments. The squeak of a squeegee on a cleaned windshield sounds like the call of a crevice-hid cricket. There is the sense that the attendant, in small but crucial ways, is looking out for us. It has to do with nostalgia for our childhoods, probably, but the transactions are no-nonsense too. Money changes hands; bills and coins get counted out. The attendant returns to his folding chair by the pumps, of a summer night; under the fluorescent lights he again takes up his neurology textbook, flicking the occasional moth off the page.

Yaquina Head

White blaps of what may be seaweed bedeck the beach at Yaquina Head, latex-looking. Or they may be scraps of a thick-skinned species of jellyfish, painful to touch, or something else entirely, the used condoms of Neptune. That would be cool. I could use an alternative to the monotony of the surf.

I could use an alternative to the art around here too. The Oregon coast is home to countless "driftwood artists," and at least one sculptress who specializes in "dog figures;" I saw her sign by the highway. Is such stuff the residue of once-great passions, as the goo on the beach implies the sea god's pleasure? What fires the imagination of the dog figure sculptress? It's hard to follow the phosphor lights in the kelp forest gloom, in the coastal fog. It is hard to find one's way.

God Lives Underwater

In Florence I overheard two couples
(Americans) discussing the unimpressive
genitals of Michelangelo's *David*.
I could have asked them if they had noticed

the *David*'s rather too-large head and hands,
the out-of-proportion parts marking him
as a Renaissance man: poised, capable,
taking Goliath's measure. Would not

a prominent putz, or a potbelly for
that matter, suggest a certain lack
of control? I could have posed these questions,
having paid attention in Art History 101,

but the four had gone on to complain at length
about President Clinton, the Big Mac-o-philic
Renaissance poonhound, who had just been elected.
"What's going to happen to us?" they bewailed.

What happened is, they left (like I did)
the café's well-stocked environs
and took another whack at the Uffizi,
drifting past the masterpieces,

trying to shed the Teflon of small talk
so an epiphany could get its pincer-like hands
on their innermost selves, to pain and tickle.
Maybe (like me) they came across the squat

figure of Priapus, he of the truly tremendous
erection, and deemed him ridiculous too.
Did they read how he used to hold sway
out of sight, underwater, bottom of a well

in Ephesus, by which barren women prayed?
Serious business, Priapus old boy,
earthbound, clay-made, full of yearning.
I won't laugh at you. Not much. I'll try to keep in mind

the contingent, cornered truth of the baby-wanting
women who begged to your beyondness.

Ditto Michelangelo's underdog of divine
cool. Ditto Slick Willie's indiscretions. Ditto the dopey
Republican couples, who must've desired
a dose of transcendence (who doesn't?), and even

myself, for in the dark I fight concurrent urges:

the one that tells me to eat too much, and the one
that tells me to hide the salaam. Oh,
there are giants one fights each day, each
night. There are giants one fights to the death.

Pique

On a jar of Marie's Piquant Tartar Sauce,
Marie herself: high heels with ankle straps,
short skirt, for contrast a small apron
and best of all the big wooden spoon

she held aloft, bossy/playful, up for anything.
Stern taskmistress, that Marie. More
complex by far than Betty or Veronica.
Absently I swabbed my fishsticks through

the processed goop, I chewed the gritty mouthfuls,
the curve of Marie's calves looking at me
quite firmly, my face reflected in the toaster
distorting monstrously, innocently. . . .

Thus my adolescence passed: I sprouted
wolfman hairs and periodically got hard
to a pixie hybrid of *Gulliver's Travels*
and *The Hite Report*. My hormones' 24/7

moaning consigned to Saturday nights, I now
understand whore is a home that fits all sizes (man,
woman, and child), the oldtime Sharkofishies (meaning
slaveships), railroad barons and descendants,

basketballers, movie stars, stalk stalk stalkers; now I am
thoroughly conversant with what Mr. Williams
meant when he said "The pure
products of America/go crazy" and Bill

Knott barked "In curtseyland I'll take my stand!"
and E. Costello asked the point blank question
"Who put these fingerprints on my imagination?;"
now is the time for me to scribble

sweet nothings in the breakfast nook,
Marie, straight to you. Let's stretch the notion
of democracy as far as it will go. Picture
a row of dominoes that fall sideways

one by one, doing no harm to the next in line;
let them become the crossties of a railroad track
horizon-rushing but arriving
never; let the rails rise and twist,

the double helix (aka DNA)
recovered from a crime scene,
binding generations. Are you still
with me, Marie? I compare all that

to the propagation of assorted noses,
predilections (including guilt), and equity
through time. Thus I come to the deeply
weird part: Who made you, Marie,

also made me. Implicated, I'm in the goop
and fizz of goods and services;
the stock market's ziggiest zag
interests me, as I must tend to the nickels

and dimes I inherited, and (Praise
the Lord) I do all right, being
fond of the Coke machine's red glow
humming outside the feed store late at night:

cold, cold (cold as advertised) cans of a sweetness
that can eat nails, the legend goes. Gratefully
I partake even though I kneejerk hate
parent corporations; that's what "piquant" means

to yours truly, Marie. I've peeked and I've peaked
and now I am pure pique, here in Crumbville,
where wanderlust is rampant. If ever I travel
to Ireland, home of my ancestors

and their famous famine, I'll keep an eye out
for a leprechaun (shillelagh, clay pipe,
as depicted) cocking an eyebrow
to signal curiosity, as actual humans
actually do.

Marquee

Mickey Rooney licking the mothdust
(possibly a hallucinogen) off a dead
lightbulb: that's how weird you can get,
how thwarted. . . .

I would be the pear-shaped
pasha of an Art Deco palace built
circa 1926, heyday of herkyjerky
black and silver movies, marquees

beat by moths, faces for the swimming in,
and light a fluid substance: glamour beyond
which we—the audience members, the wannabes—
become amoebas, subdivisioning lacklustrously

our tuneless, ever tinnier selves.
Hermaphroditic, harumphing at everything,
yet wistful. . . . Thoughts like static. . . .
Depressing, yes?

Look, Lilliputianed by TV, in the wee hours
there's Lana Turner the owl-faced ingenue
phosphorescing in a white swimsuit
for John Garfield. His glass jaw

McCarthy's just about to sock.
Why not enlarge on that?

I would sit alone in the back row
and synchronize my breathing with the others'.
Our flaring nostrils would homage the
obvious, an oversize kiss like a gyroscope,

oscillating. In Spanish "to kiss"
is "oscular;" that ab ovos the motion I mean.
Sheik condoms are named for Valentino's
character, you know? And no one,

in thoughts luminous as famous swimsuits or in
Day-Glo flags of language, would semaphore a doubt
about the whole hillfolk scenario of sitting together
Saturday nights, beholden to our betters,

our biggers. It's a wonderful life,
more or less. One wants to be bright,
one needs to be dim. Off and on,
pain takes fire inside the stray cliché

and thus unnumbed one cogitates, one feels,
one dreams. Reals within reels. In cartoons a lightbulb
means a thought, right? On a marquee
quasi-spiders of wire filaments get

fierce about their quarantine, they get
white-hot. Nearer, My Moth, to Thee.

Night Needles, Haystack Days

Famous needle, famous haystack. But I
don't need to hunt, I have my loves
and hates. Heartward, always, rides
the needle on the rapids of my blood.

That's how my mind runs, from bloodstream to rapids
to a river so calm you can count the stars, the needle
a canoe that holds a boy wending toward
the brights of Oz, eager to charm

the large-toothed influentials
and find a place among them.
Outside the city, naturally, a prison;
inmates lacking contacts, power;

a needle backed by order of the state
with bye-bye juices, including one to freeze
the facial muscles, so a man appears
already vacant, giving up the ghost. Needle

in a haystack indeed.
All will be hidden.
All will be revealed.
Meantime,

I'll keep rooting for the eager boy,
though I enjoy my slack-jawed moments.
As when Kathy and I stepped outside
the parent-teacher conference, feeling

hopeful, only a little pained. Our boy had
a little bad luck the day he was born,
or before. Maybe in the womb water
an iridescent devil with a fish's tail

nipped the network of his nerves, so friendship's
foreign to him. He dislikes eye
contact. He's different. The sky
and the stone church across the street,

when we stepped outside the school, were not
different, meeting nearly seamlessly, the same
bluegray, stopping us there. Then
we walked on, talking about the weather.

Then the restaurant, chunks of apple
in a green salad. Then I got up to take a leak
and a loner with a shaved head snorted at me
and shook his headshine at my white-fuzzed mouse-

pink pate, unbrotherly, to say the least, arousing
in me the petty rage I'm famous for.
In kindergarten I tried to kill a hamster
that had bitten me! I had to be restrained. That's

my life, a common one: church and sky can blend, a bluegray
to shame the bluegrayest hydrangea, and just
like that a grown man gets mad enough
to squash a hamster in one hand. But

it is our luck that such picayune states pass.
The cloud-roiled sky clears, indigo, a good clear dark,
the church recedes to a thing apart,
the myriad needles begin to shine

above, the glims and the shivs alike. Each
night aesthete angels with needle teeth
and glitter-mad goblins face off. Night comes
and it is our luck, if no one ever finds us.

Magnetic Fields in a Galaxy of Mutants

Salt caves in New Mexico with creeping
exactitude, crystal by crystal, surround
canisters of Cold War nuclear waste,
sealing off the heebie-jeebies; centuries will pass

suchways. Once upon a time I scraped
beneath the kitchen table a fat magnet
to make iron filings (topside) do my bidding:
bristle, lean, lie down, be still. They stood

like soldiers, they sprouted like a corpse's beard,
they froze the fluxlines of repulsion
and attraction. And Saturn's gee-whiz rings
(I read this book to my child, a five year-old boy

with a willful streak like a frozen river through
warm-looking brown fields, a mouthbreather
who mutters spells against his parents; his blondbrown
hair grows soft as duck feathers)—Saturn's rings are in

reality ice and rocks whirling round—hunks the size
of the house we live in; flotsams fingernail-tiny,
flickering—prismatic, perfect, just near enough. So
one must hold with the hidden forces.

A Charcoal Drawing in a Children's Book

I spied, I spent time with a charcoal drawing
(derivative) inside a vintage children's book—

Depression era droopezoid shapes
slung over the branches of witchy trees

and the pointy parts of Gothic shacks,
as though the melting moon were dropping

on everything great blobs of nuclear butter—
a Salvador Dalí done by an empty stomach.

The drawing drips nostalgia, the shadows feel
like home. Which the smothered sharpnesses despise.

In My Dream About the Iditarod

I'm dead last, loonylonesome, heartstab-aware of my dad
reading aloud "The Cremation of Sam McGee" long ago.
He used to laugh so hard the tears would start.
And in my dream I yap at the halfwolf dogs
of sparkleland, I yap for the dead to come back.

In My Dream After Thanksgiving Dinner with My Wife's Family

My mother-in-law, walnut-colored from Mazatlán,
scarcely audible, natters on and on
about what coupons she has clipped
and it sounds like a list of my sins.

Man Doing His Taxes

Under a gooseneck lamp
in an otherwise dim room, white hands,

knob-knuckled. The bags under his eyes
vibrate faintly with fatigue. Now I see:

it's my dad. He taught me how to work:
that glaring light, those shadowy bruises.

I Was Right

My brother, when he couldn't afford
paints, used to busy his hands

by carving minute naked women
out of bars of Ivory soap

and they even had nipples. And I
thought to myself "Man, that's art."

A Dog Hungry for Bones, Our Happiness

The Angel of Death puts an eyehole to the keyhole
covetously, old stackabones—he would touch himself
if he had a body to touch—but inside with us our
watchdog slobberskeins with his God-given tongue
the keyhole shut.

Gargoyles

I saw a twentysomething *Twilight* star
doing something with his face:
pouting to be handsome.

How stupid. Let's emphasize instead
the orgasm, so democratic
it gargoyles every face.

The Beatles' White LP Record Album vs. "Your Catfish Friend" by Richard Brautigan

The best Beat proser (Kerouac), who
allowed "Women are the crocodilefolk,"
solaced me once upon a time.

A 104-pound hottie, C cup, she
teased me mercilessly in college.
(After her I got bad grades, because I

could not concentrate.) New feeling: I felt
proud how pretty she was. I talked
too much. I said many

silly things, and she did not smirk,
she did not sniff. She listened.

Once, pretending not to hear me,
she tucked her hair behind her ear
and bit her lip. Sexy. Turns out she was

fucking a construction worker
a couple times a week. When I found out,
I took the keys out of the ignition,

threw them onto the roof of a house,
and (second worst thing I ever said)
said "Fetch."

(Before that, in the car, I had cast a phosphorescent
green laserbeam of a fishing line
down to the little white trout she was, the climax—at least

for me—to the whole affair, spontaneous conflation:
"He can just fuck you in the ear." So what?)

Egg on the Step, Pettiest Thing I Ever Did

An enthusiast (VISIONS OF CODY, ON THE ROAD) I felt like
I was everywhere, mild weather
Hallowe'en Day. Working a big wad of bubblegum
with my jaw (a huge wad—I had gotten into
the Hallowe'en candy, I was happy),
I crossed the street, and Boone my mighty coonhound
pulled hard on the leash. I blew
a bubble, popped it. I saw an old man
sitting alone at his kitchen table and I
waved friendlily at him. Why not?
In response he made the whoop-de-doo gesture
(a sort of whirlwind with one hand, a vertical
version of the crazy gesture). I decided
to egg his house that night (though I love
the Tennessee Williams quote "Deliberate
unkindness is the greatest sin"). The hours
passed. I procured one egg—white as white
can be, slightly pebbled—from the fridge.
My wife (as if endowed with ESP
or witchly intuition) said, looking
worried, "What are you doing?"
"Nothing." I walked to the old man's
house, chickened out (the sound of a splat
might bring him to the window), and
set the egg on his front step
to frighten him, maybe, or simply
to make him aware of an entity
(possibly benign, possibly sadistic) aware
of him. Such is life on Earth. It was
not my place to worry him. For years
afterward I found scraps of
eggshells in my yard, as if blown there
by the wind, or carried there
by rats, little by little
making me a Christian neighbor.

Worst Thing I Ever Said

18 or 19, I build a little fire
at the foot of a big Douglas fir
in my back yard, the better
to ruminate about Kezia Brooks,
a nearly albino girl I find
attractive, who never looks back.
Two friends, not close ones, show up:
Rich the Bitch and Brian Henton.
There's the whiteness of a bone
in the bridge of Rich's big nose, as if
it's about to break the skin. It,
and he, annoy me. I feel sorry
for Brian because his brother has
a football scholarship to Stanford, plus
Brian seems not smart to me (save
for the great nickname he gave himself:
"Tug." "Because all the women want to tug
on my dick"). Then he laughs alone,
theatrically, at his own greatness.
He laughs like the dumbass he is
till I, quiet by nature, say something
that ends the friendship: "Ah, the same
rich laughter that once echoed
across the plantations." Silence. Rich
bugs his eyes, then laughs. Brian laughs
too, vehemently kicking out the campfire
of my revery. Pissed, I stare. Surprise:
the next day Brian's father calls mine.
Despite Mr. Henton's high dudgeon, Dad says
tersely "My son is not a racist" and hangs up. Sorry,
Old Tug. My dad and I are born romantics.

E-mailing Allen Iverson

Dear Mr. Iverson (aka
"The Answer," franchise
player with a little trouble
at the mansion—sirens,
flashing lights—a handgun tucked
under his baggy shirt, incongruously
beautiful brown eyes,
a small body
by NBA standards,
who nonetheless ranks
high on the all-time
fouls drawn list,
who is fearless
on the job): What
do your tattoos
mean?

And you,
Lebron James, arms festooned
like a Maori warrior's,
do you fear
the police too?
Are you paranoid
like me?
Are you friends
with Warren Buffet?
Lebron, best ever
to play the game
perhaps (6' 8", 250),
a prodigy
smart
and strong and quick
largely because God

made you so,
who works hard, whose
teammates respect him—
Mayor of Akron, No
Jawbone of an Ass—
I love
your laser passes,
just about everybody
loves you—
whose game
requires
less courage than mine.

Wild Kingdom

As a boy I was embarrassed by
Appaloosas, for
they all have spotted rumps.
Later on, my first blowjob,

I worried it hurt the woman's neck.
(She also taught me about
Anarchy and tittiecentric egotism,
alas.) But what I want to talk about

is the opening montage of the TV show
Wild Kingdom circa 1968. I watched it
out of the corner of my eye,
from the dinner table. Shots of animals

being animals: a cheetah running
topspeed (70 mph, it's said). I liked the cheetah.
Then (blatant racism, in the wake of Selma marches)
to end the intro, a shot of an African native

in a loincloth and a feathered headdress,
dancing. His skin was almost purple,
shiny with sweat. He made me
so queasy I could not eat.

Was I a racist? Maybe. Was I scared of sex? Yes.

Peace Corps Volunteer

I.

It's Indian Summer in Peyton Place.
Two white people with goose pimples
go skinnydipping despite the daylight.

Naptime a woman puts a goofball
on her tongue. *Glub glub glub,* she gazes
up.

II.

I recall a split-rail fence
to keep out a species
of diminutive deer, reddish brown
with white spots. . . .

I used to dose my water with quinine
for its timeless aluminum undertaste. . . .
I saw my future in an ice cube
I held up to the sky

like a glass model of a hominid skull
or the dog-chewed head of a Barbie doll
amusing the Smithsonian. . . .

Speaking of fences: Honest
Abe, Railsplitter Abe walked five miles
to return a book he'd read by firelight.
Good man.

Then the White House bathed in moonlight.

There God tormented. The President
fretted, freed the slaves. . . .
Juneteenth Day his wife went crazy.

That's the story of my life:
Ma reading MANDINGO, FALCONHURST FANCY, DRUM;
Ma enjoying Spike Lee's feature-length

debut *She's Gotta Have It* (some angry
sex in that one); Ma reading half
THE AUTOBIOGRAPHY OF MALCOLM X before

she died.

First word in Malcolm's dictionary
and in mine: Aardvark.
One world led to another. Ma'd forget a few
cups of cold tea and wadded-up Kleenex

around the house. I'd disappear
them now and then. Poor Ma,
pacing.

Two purple spats of blood like an English starling's
blackberry-juice-and-seeds shit in the stainless steel
kitchen sink the night of Ma's most serious
suicide attempt. (Never phone for help
on such a night. The cops keep the note.)

Signed: Love, Mom.

Why do I write? You can't
keep a good man down.

A work crew must've slashed and burned some jungle.
A child must've burrowed his hand in some soft white ashes,
fine soft ashes, a wisp swirling up. . . .

Alone for a time I tended my Xigua patch
in Cameroon, sweating, anxious because the sharp bills
squawked and the carnivores huffed.

Pomegranate

I.

Adam and Eve, coffee-colored people,
lolled on their bellies listening to waterfalls,
toucan squawks, and dinner always something
tasty (say pomegranate and trout). Lacking

tanlines, each found the slightly lighter
skin of the other's eyelids lovely,
such featherweight striations. (Dawn:
gradual and of great subtlety its

pinks and grays, because Seraphim
pussyfoot, kneading the night away.)
Eve's eyelids were gazed upon most intently
when she looked over her shoulder

with her eyes closed. Adam also beheld
what Shahrazad spoke: "When she smiles,
the corners of her eyes touch her ears."
My wife has green eyes and rather large ears,

so large in fact they poke through her hair.
She looks like a mouse. All the beasts of Eden leap
and crawl, and the rarest quality in the raucous land—
the Serpent's talk by comparison a used car salesman's—

the rarest, subtlest quality, tenderness,
of many facets and azure toothpaste breath,
of eyelids pale as lichen and ears
turned pink by the setting sun.

Our son used to haul himself up
to the windowsill and wobble, watching

for his mother to get home from work.
The sky, charcoal swathes and streaks of red:

that's when the light would turn his ears pink
and I would want to gobble him up!
I wanted to gobble up his mother too!
Me, I'm the hog-wild Tickle Monster, roaring.

Any notion of paradise that includes
a cracked-open pomegranate (seeds seeds seeds)
must also include that feeling, that greed
to grab the beloveds and hold them too tight.

It's nuts, of course. It's called "possessive." But
it's the star-crossed, stupid best I can do for them,
flesh of my flesh (crack their ribs and go
kiss kiss kiss) when I get that itch:

a prickle, a premonition:
one white pinfeather spiraling
down from the Angel of Death
to tickle the back of one's neck.

II.

Mustn't forget the rest of the story.
Mustn't forget the Tree of Knowledge,
the Flaming Sword, and the Sweat of One's Brow.
Mustn't forget the other feelings, like pride and hate.

Nomads (herdsmen like Abel) still haughty, ad
hominem, to the hunkerdowns (farmers like Cain),
the hunkerdowns hating their trampled crops.
And if you take brother-against-brother to the Nth

degree, random hoofprints rebuking blithely
crops in rows, then the whole shebang
proceeds from bad to worse: the passing-throughs
vs. the property-holders, the tramplers
vs. the tenders. Where's paradise now?

There are islands where scarcely anyone lives,
there are pages glossy as tropical foliage. And
Fletcher Christian's most fetching descendant Darlene
(bucktoothed) does grin at me from the pages
of ARCHAEOLOGY magazine, the Bounty

tattooed on her shoulderblade in blue ink.
You've heard about the famous mutiny
but what about Christian being murdered
years later by a jealous Polynesian husband?
What's the story there? In the picture

Darlene's mixed blood seems to be
at peace. And me, my ethnicity's prone to
freckling, to pinkness, but my wife gets brown.
"God" is a word that gets said. God. As always,
paradise plays out in private, in shades, with
tenderness and rules for violence between

the bodies. And it happens sometimes
that a person will murmur "Is that nice?
Is that nice?" But not nice is better. Not talking
is better, because the bodies bioluminesce.
They beam like the audience at a minstrel show.

Hotplate as Agent of Nostalgia and Old Man's Companion

Big fight with my wife
for the umpteenth time,
acrimony, contempt.
Fuck it.
I'll go get an apartment and a hotplate
and write poems.
But I stay.

Mainly I stay because our son
(mildly autistic) makes up
words like "pretensiologist"
and "Marxmas" (everybody gets the same thing).
Neon, for our family, neologisms.

When he reaches college age, his
mom and I may break up. Her family
has money. I'll be poor.
I'll heat up soup on my hotplate,
concocting poems partly out of
words the kid created.
I'll stare into space,
less happy than I am now,
remembering.

I may recall grayish cartoons
by Ben Katchor. He wrote about
old people, conscious of
their sorrowing, their monthly checks
the opposite of lip gloss, of adolescence.

Masten's Variety: a bin of dusty
jawbreakers I saw long ago intrigued me.
Where did they come from?

How were they made?
(Oxymoron: candy that hurts.)

In one Katchor cartoon
a truckload of lipsticks
overturns, leaving
a red
Rita Hayworth smear on
a highway in New Jersey.
(The Information Superhighway's
nowhere to be seen.)
Red's in my mind,
gray's on the page.

Katchor, all he was after
was a pang of
nostalgia
made possible by small companies.
Sweet man.

Ma put on red red lipstick
before she left the house.
Also a scarf. Old-fashioned.
Ma made good gravy,
I wiped it up with white bread.
I loved her fourth best
on my walk around the world,
my father second,
my son first.

Memories of Johnny Weismuller's Pectoral Muscles Soothe Me After My Wife's Double Mastectomy

A competent, probably happy cameraman
filmed one of the Depression's entertainments:
Johnny Weismuller
swimming the sunlit underwaterways
of Florida, hexagons of waterlight wobbling
the sandy creek bottoms. Intercut
non-Hollywood footage of crocodiles
scrabbling speedily the banks of the Nile,
splashing for my semi-excitement.

In quiet moments Johnny Weismuller's
junglated nonswimming pectoral muscles
troubled me.
They seemed too large, too feminine.

He lived in a tree with a woman
as sharp-featured and strategically-adiposed
as the woman who lives across the street
from me, who never says hi. When she
draws the curtains to breastfeed her baby,
I see the wicked wrinkling of her nose.
What does she read in the evenings?

I thought the face of
my ninth grade Marine Biology teacher
Mr. Taylor
animalistic, eager, and kind.
He scuba dived.
He had hair like Johnny Weismuller's:
wet, slicked back black hair, with
a flop of wet black forelock
and a gap between his front teeth

to indicate passion. The most heavy-lidded
of dunderheads respected him.

One summer day Mr. Taylor, working at the feed store,
slung a 100 lb. sack of rock salt
off his shoulder, into the back of my Mazda.
It seems the cook at the Steak House,
where I washed dishes, needed
100 lbs. of rock salt to tenderize
the Prime Rib Special for our boozy patrons
and their Coke-sipping offspring. Great Caesar's Ghost
and Gadzooks, it was a good surprise to see you
again, ugly-handsome Mr. Taylor, turtlenecked
and stevedorish. Strong. Back
at the restaurant, unloading the bag of rock salt
like a dead body, I felt wimpy in my
bloodsmeared white shirt, in the wrong line of work.

You were a fine teacher, Mr. Taylor, far
underpaid. My lucky break, they appointed me Assistant Professor
to the blue and orange of Sear Accuse.
I was considered sensitive.
Intuitive.

One weekend, three weeks into the grinding of my molars,
my wife and I swam alone
in a motel pool only 5 feet deep
and I, popping up, exclaimed
"Underwater otter adventure!"
I was so happy to be away
from the intrigues of the court eunuchs,
not the students.

Why couldn't I be one of the walrus-shaped firemen,
pornostached, in Hornell town for the firemen's convention?
Why couldn't I save someone's life?

Life wasn't all bad.
Here's a rule I laid down for myself:
Only teach poems you love.

Once the vice president of the liars' club
made me cry on the phone.

Years later my wife's incomparable silver dollarsize pink
areolas got petri dished and described in an objective way.
She works at a bookstore. No reconstructive surgery
for her, no bra with fake kabongas, no
sir. Concave-chested, big-tummied as a
baby cuckoo bird in another bird's nest,
she wears an Incredible Hulk T-shirt that reads
MY BOYFRIEND IS INCREDIBLE
which, she claims, refers to me.

For me the good life means
lying in bed late at night
and sort of watching a bygone era's
black-and-silver movies, and worrying
about metastases.

(One night the Lord whipped up the Spirit of Lilith
especially for me, as punishment perhaps,
the Spirit of a Woman in a hoop skirt,
red-haired. She swirled into the room
and leaned over me. Was she someone I had
obsessed about or bewarted, or the one I abandoned?
Accompaniment: the sound of rushing wind.
Briefly terrifying, that sound, her sallow face.)

But I always wake up to two cups of coffee
and the sign of the Cross
and, God willing, another good scribble.

What the good life means to my wife
I inquire obliquely, from time
to time, as in "Good morning."

African Jelly Beans

Truth be told,
my best girlfriend was named Miss Wright.
Kismet. An English major.
A frothiness. Knowledge of pink nipples.

18 years later
my Chinese psychiatrist says
"You're dealing with deep levels of your mind."
No tenses down there. The present.

Movie night,
20,000 Leagues Under the Silent Version,
James Mason's black glistening Shug
Knight Beard is also a thing of beauty.
But enough about that.

Co-dependent, Jacques Cousteau pouring a capful of bleach
into the octopus's bucket to amuse Philippe,
I count on Henry to take apart with tweezers
my conspiracy theories.

Elsewhere a Great Horned Owl
coughs up a gray furball.
They sterilize it with hot steam
and guarantee it free of the hanta virus.

Then we pull it apart.
We count the tiny teeth in a tiny mandible
and realize it all used to be parts of a rat.
God's Precision German Engineering,
His Gray Fur Frothiness. Before us,
on the table, a forest.

Mouths in Hell

I.

Unprecedented: a leg cramp so bad I yelled a scream,
I screamed a yellow. It went on much longer
than I expected. Why did I scream
like a Girl Scout giving birth to Prometheus?

I could not help myself.
(Maybe in Eternity no sound comes out
the open mouth.)
I felt silly and ashamed, not guilty,

afterwards. A pussy. Crybaby cum laude.
In Arab countries there's shame, which
comes from the community, whereas guilt
comes from within. Which burns worse?

Shame's a Tiki torch compared to the furnace
of guilt. Schizophrenic, I read a comic
book in which the Spectre visits
a bankrobber in Hell, and it looked about right:

an endless orange conflagration, all
the souls with wide open mouths.
(Is my crime too heinous to
name, or imaginary? No.)

II.

Let's say a convict's crime
is oral rape in prison. (Heaven is full of women
and children, for they rarely rape
or murder anyone.)

Joe Wenderoth—I'm paraphrasing—says God's
angels rape one's mind from time to time
and sometimes one smiles, sometimes
one cries, sometimes one closes one's eyes. . . .

Often on his bunk the convict
spits on his palm, his solitude,
and lets his mind wander
from someone to someone. . . .

Once upon a time this man
placed a fish in a fellow inmate's mouth,
arousing onlookers, hating the fish. . . .

The color blue is solitude.
The color blue is confusing.
The color blue is heaven for you.

The Everlasting Appeal of the Supernatural

Not merely at murder
scenes with their mess

of essential and non-
essential hieroglyphs

say a concrete windowsill
with bloody trifurcations

pigeon tracks which must
have made a sound

as of struck matches
leading the eye skyward

but also at lethal injections
the State orchestrates

mouse-demeanored
MUTE-buttoned there's mystery

minus its haystack
a needle

naked as the Cross
after Christ

flew the coop spooky
too like the caduceus

two snakes endrape—
birdwings bedizen the sky

beyond cobalt the coldest
possible blue

My Right Wrist's Ornate Celtic Cross Tattoo (4" x 2 1/2") Almost Covers the Three Pink Scars

I.

Each eye a mouth.

Venus flytrap eyes, on each eyelash tip
a bright drop of toxin . . .

Meat the 666 trap. Saint Peter sees
the trap shut.

The bright spikes bring Jesus.
"Bright Spear," etymologically, "Lucifer."

II.

Quaking red of the cough syrup
convex
on the spoon, for the cough robs
the household of sleep.

For the cough torments the child.

The various coagulations of thought,
they stick to the floor.

Reaching man's hand a doorknob distorts,
then the hand rests. He is listening.

Thud-thud his heart does, but in this room
the thief is the heart of the matter.

A church bell's tongue wrapped in a towel.
A skull wearing a fortuneteller's turban.

Torment
God makes possible.

This the bad dream's
banishing, switch the lightswitch off.

Hear the child's breathing?

III.

"We come to faith by hearing."
Hear the end of wretchedness:

The severed ear of the soldier seamlessly restored.
Peter's bloody car restored askew.

How Many Angels Can Dance on the Head of a Pin?

I.

SABHAL, Gaelic, "barn."
See that banshee by the barn?

Stick a needle in my eye.
Cross my heart and hope to die.

Black-souled, a beast glossy as black
ink, I promise to tell you the truth.

II.

Better-than-Muzak Jesus message at the threshold
of audibility: heaven heaven heaven. . . .

Multitudinous small gray moths
beating their wings, coming close
one by one. . . .

"In" said an angel, sticking
a pin in my eye. Goodnight.

III.

Buddyboy, you have no power to send me to Hell.
Pussycats like you crucified me.

After the exegesis the glossary.
After the nails the good dream:

Gollum leads the Balrog away
on the finest chain you've

ever let pool upon one wrist. . . .
Amen, amanuensis, amen.

7Up for an Upset Stomach in Saipan

Where is our story set? Where is your best memory? On
Wizard Island All Covered With Wyssen And Moss.

Why?
Because I read Duns Scotus as a child.
(Duns Scotus believed the will more important
Than the intellect, disagreeing with Aquinas.)

Where's the lustrous-handed, wispily hirsute thief?
A thrift store in Des Moines.
Fan of Black Pudding, Dungeons and Dragons.
Not smart.

Do you remember Dunsmuir? Yes.
Maniacal laughter from the courtyard.
Our room: pelvic thrust, involuntary sound.
Giddyup, giddyup. Slavering wolves, evergreens.
·Rivendell, but our souls were squashed as dwarves.
The cannabis scent of her hair
Lent to the proceedings a sweetness.

Finally, I became a father.
An octopus climbed a large-boled tree,
A Garry Oak in Smith Park, Oak Harbor.

A Chammoro mom gave her daughter
7Up for an upset stomach.
Scar above the girl's right eye.
Dog attack.
One quarter I taught that young woman nothing.
Wondrously confident and calm she was in person.
She wrote clearly.

Five years later I see her Facebook posts:
"Island Girl."
"Sir Nathan finds these sardines subpar."
"My son is not so much snoring as grunting.
He seems to be disapproving his dream."
Nathan is three. His mom also posts
An article about "Literary Manboys."

Meanwhile,
A MOBY-DICK school project
Made by my twelve year-old:
Queequeg's coffin a shoebox painted brown.
Inside, a ship in a bottle.
Outside, Post-its of his favorite lines.
Maori patterns, black ink visible against the brown.

Henry's interested in the South Seas.
Breadfruit trees.
Rumors of cannabalism.
A box of bones the pointy teeth
Feel awkward about.
Story of the Spirit House:
"Three go in, two come out."

My son likes scarification. Dot dot dot.
Maori whorls, maps of labyrinths.
A whorl would be an ear,
An ear to catch the world.

Here's how Henry lives:
He listens to the palm fronds flail
And sussurate, a warm wind-blown
Warm rain in Hawaii.
Harmless. Kind.
Not like me. Not like mental illness.

What happened to his tiny Guatamalan Worry Dolls?
He lost them.
I made one of my own out of earwax
But it melted on a chipped windowsill.

That's how my true love and I often were:
Worried, uncommunicative. Cozy basement.
James Franco
Smiled, "Glinfendor the Thief,"
Last episode of a TV series we liked.

You understand the greennesses
The Spring rains accentuate.
As if the soft rains chartreusify our sufferings.
It's very sad and then again it's almost unbearable.
Highlight your favorite Bible passage.
God understands our everythings.

My love wanted to do the Eskimo blanket toss
For our baby's second birthday
But being introverted I gave her
A glum maybe.

Let's not go
To Europe again, big old
Disneyland it is.
Neuschwanstein: New Swanstone.
On the tour a British kid asked, last thing,
"Are we going to see the torture chamber?"

Think of Emily imprisoned in her paradoxes.

This is how Jesus explains Heaven to the thief,
"I will be with you today."

A Quahog for Walt

"'The time has come,' the Walrus said."

How many inscrutable angels does it take to screw in
a lightbulb? None.

How many mice?
Two, but there's not much room.

Two of Ma's favorite expressions:
"It smelled like low tide at Coney Island."
"She looked like the last whore at the clambake."

One of Dad's expressions:
"Your ass is grass."
Jump the fence, Johnson grass can cut your feet.

Pisser clams seem nonplussed by my poems,
I'm volatile as a quahog in public.

I'm quiet at home too.
We eat, and are grateful.

Night, my head hits the pillow.
Night, I pray my gratitude
and a little fluid leaks out of my left ear,
relieving the pain. Lilac. Saguaro. Dandelion.

Author's Note

The Middle Ages is an unusual book in that the poems written before the poet's break with reality are markedly different from those written after. (There was a three-year silence in-between the writing of the two groups of poems.) See if you can tell which poems are which.

Acknowledgments

Grateful acknowledgment is made to the following publications, in whose pages these poems first appeared:

Alaska Quarterly Review, "Magnetic Fields in a Galaxy of Mutants"

Fine Madness, "Buffalo Commons, Century 21"

Forklift, Ohio, "Oregon's Gas Station Attendants" and "Yaquina Head"

The Kenyon Review, "Fishing for Perch" and "The Middle Age"

Like Never Before, "The Middle Age"

110, "Swandive"

Poets for Living Waters, "A Quahog for Walt"

T88A Journal, "Road Trip"

Verse Daily, "The Middle Age"

About the Author

The Middle Ages is Roger Fanning's third book of poems. He lives in Seattle with his wife and son.

PENGUIN POETS

JOHN ASHBERY
Selected Poems
Self-Portrait in a Convex
  Mirror

TED BERRIGAN
The Sonnets

LAUREN BERRY
The Lifting Dress

JOE BONOMO
Installations

PHILIP BOOTH
Selves

JIM CARROLL
Fear of Dreaming: The Selected
  Poems
Living at the Movies
Void of Course

ALISON HAWTHORNE DEMING
Genius Loci
Rope

CARL DENNIS
Callings
New and Selected Poems
  1974–2004
Practical Gods
Ranking the Wishes
Unknown Friends

DIANE DI PRIMA
Loba

STUART DISCHELL
Backwards Days
Dig Safe

STEPHEN DOBYNS
Velocities: New and Selected
  Poems, 1966–1992

EDWARD DORN
Way More West: New and
  Selected Poems

ROGER FANNING
The Middle Ages

ADAM FOULDS
The Broken Word

CARRIE FOUNTAIN
Burn Lake

AMY GERSTLER
Crown of Weeds: Poems
Dearest Creature
Ghost Girl
Medicine
Nerve Storm

EUGENE GLORIA
Drivers at the Short-Time Motel
Hoodlum Birds

DEBORA GREGER
Desert Fathers, Uranium
  Daughters
God
Men, Women, and Ghosts
Western Art

TERRANCE HAYES
Hip Logic
Lighthead
Wind in a Box

ROBERT HUNTER
Sentinel and Other Poems

MARY KARR
Viper Rum

WILLIAM KECKLER
Sanskrit of the Body

JACK KEROUAC
Book of Sketches
Book of Blues
Book of Haikus

JOANNA KLINK
Circadian
Raptus

JOANNE KYGER
As Ever: Selected Poems

ANN LAUTERBACH
Hum
If in Time: Selected Poems,
  1975–2000
On a Stair
Or to Begin Again

CORINNE LEE
PYX

PHILLIS LEVIN
May Day
Mercury

WILLIAM LOGAN
Macbeth in Venice
Strange Flesh
The Whispering Gallery

ADRIAN MATEJKA
Mixology

MICHAEL MCCLURE
Huge Dreams: San Francisco
  and Beat Poems

DAVID MELTZER
David's Copy: The Selected
  Poems of David Meltzer

ROBERT MORGAN
Terroir

CAROL MUSKE-DUKES
An Octave above Thunder
Red Trousseau
Twin Cities

ALICE NOTLEY
Culture of One
The Descent of Alette
Disobedience
In the Pines
Mysteries of Small Houses

LAWRENCE RAAB
The History of Forgetting
Visible Signs: New and Selected
  Poems

BARBARA RAS
The Last Skin
One Hidden Stuff

MICHAEL ROBBINS
Alien vs. Predator

PATTIANN ROGERS
Generations
Wayfare

WILLIAM STOBB
Absentia
Nervous Systems

TRYFON TOLIDES
An Almost Pure Empty Walking

ANNE WALDMAN
Kill or Cure
Manatee/Humanity
Structure of the World
  Compared to a Bubble

JAMES WELCH
Riding the Earthboy 40

PHILIP WHALEN
Overtime: Selected Poems

ROBERT WRIGLEY
Beautiful Country
Earthly Meditations: New and
  Selected Poems
Lives of the Animals
Reign of Snakes

MARK YAKICH
The Importance of Peeling
  Potatoes in Ukraine
Unrelated Individuals Forming
  a Group Waiting to Cross

JOHN YAU
Borrowed Love Poems
Paradiso Diaspora